Mesa Verde, Colorado, May 2017

Egocentricity: Time Spin

Poems by

Phyllis Ann Shaw, Ph.D.

Egocentricity: Time Spin

Copyright © 2017 by Phyllis Ann Shaw, Ph.D.

First edition

ISBN: 978-0-692-88623-6

For my parents Annie Mildred Bayliss and John Pete ("Bud") Wright, Jr., who instilled in their family the value of education, truth, and most of all love.

Comments

"This deep and moving volume is a valuable addition to the genre of narrative poetry. Dr. Shaw's honesty and raw emotion shines throughout the collection. I was transported to a place of quiet reflection."

Jill Maura Rabin, M.D.

"Phyllis was born in a tiny town in Arkansas, right on the border with Oklahoma and close to Texas. Her family moved often during her childhood. She obtained a bachelor's degree at a liberal arts college in Sherman, Texas, and a MS and PhD at the University of Texas Graduate School of Biomedical Sciences in Houston, followed by a post-doctoral fellowship at Columbia University in New York City. She is a highly respected scientist and teacher, a tenured professor at the Icahn School of Medicine at Mount Sinai in Manhattan. Phyllis is through and through a scientist, but there's a poet in there too, wanting to speak to us, with important things to say. We should listen."

Susan Kaiser, Ph.D., M. D.

Phyllis Ann Shaw movingly describes a life in these poems, a life that blossomed through "the growing pain of growing." As she notes, "things ... / cannot remain constant." With empathy, she meditates over life's moments and comes to share valuable lessons for the receptive reader. It is apt—and believable—that she ends her collection by sharing, "it has been told / ... that things of gold / glitter // but I find / that other things shine." Phyllis, herself, shines with these poems.

— *Eileen R. Tabios, Poet*

This is a collection of poems written in the 1960s and 1970s, very tumultuous times. They are personal reflections of the external tumult and its effect on the internal longings, dreams and disappointments of a very young person. In deciding to publish them today, I meant to evoke those times for the generation that was born much later and into a new and different era. They cover a broad range of human experiences that my students who read them assure me are relevant today.

pas, 30 May, 2017

Acknowledgements

Thank you to my family (and there are many of them!), Chantal, Jill (and family), Caroline (and family) and Sue K. for all their love, support, and encouragement. Also thank you Phoebe, Lucy G., Anna, Allison, Danny, Adam, Lewis, Lucy O'S., Sylvia, and Slavena, who motivated me to publish, and to all of the medical students who keep me young!

I am especially grateful to my dear friend Lilly, who carefully read my poems (many times), made many helpful suggestions, and edited the final copy.

Thank you to David Creed with whom I wrote one of the poems.

Drawings by:

Benjamin Crable, "Love"

Lucy O'Shaughnessy, "Reflection", Heartbreak", "Whimsy", and those scattered throughout the rest of the poems. Thank you very much!

Thank you Nick Maj for formatting the book.

Contents

Love   **9**

Reflections   **35**

Heartbreak   **61**

Whimsy   **85**

Love

my heart quickens
at the thought of you...
your eyes penetratingly soft

my body longs
for the touch of yours...
smooth and responsively warm

my eyes long
to look at you and be

enraptured

pas, 10 April, 1969

as the sandpiper waits for the receding tide, so do i
wait my love
his eyes sift the sand, my glance is blank--my eyes do
not see
surrounded by beauty we feel only need

wait...
wait for time to pass
a relationship to end
in hopes that another will begin

the sandpiper is more practical
he waits for food
a reality

surrounded by plenty we both feel hunger

pas, 27 April, 1969

i miss you

there must be some particular spot in my heart that
you fill
some particular thought that gives me a quiet thrill

it is not a feeling of loneliness or incompleteness
but more one of nearness, of sweetness

wonder if it will ever be true

that for a while i will walk beside you

this is not another name for emptiness

i feel complete

or have i looked at the same thing

from the other side of the street

pas, 13 May, 1969

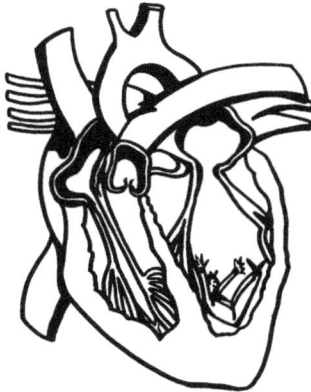

and i have walked on fields of clover

crushing not the petals 'neath my feet

and i have wandered into forests
fearing not the dangers of the deep

and i have loved in clover
forests
and all over

but thick clover and dark forests

do not make

love

less

shallow

pas, 17 July, 1969

soul sans soul
we search
for that place
where no one ever treads

heart sans heart
we long for those many
we will never know

mouth sans words
we grope
for those words
no one ever says

person to person
we
exist

pas, 24 July, 1969

my mind runs on one track

like a tv
with only
one channel

daring to go on
wanting to look
back

the track
the channel
is
you

pas, 30 July, 1969

born of feel
touch
of fingertipped skin

lotiony smooth touch
slick, slippery touch
difficult to grasp touch
hard to hold –clutch

born of satin
of reflection

mirage —
mod podge

pas, 11 February, 1970

in the hollow that is my mind
your image remains
forever impressed

after such a long time
it seems as if you
would no longer be recalled

but instead be replaced
by someone new

such is not the case

for in the hollow that is my mind
your image lives

forever

pas, 19 June, 1970

the world revolves
around revolving
lives are spent
solving the revolving

he comes, she goes
missing only that part
she says cry, cry for me
he retorts die, die for me
together they scream silence

once upon a life
there was a time
when a beautiful princess
died from a kiss
he called it love

did she call it bliss

pas, 27 July, 1972

and what of love
he cried in his anxiety

what is love

they answered vehemently

he found he had
no answer

pas, 7 August, 1973

what should i do
other than love you

i could destroy the feeling
having done so at another time
it is easier now

however
i see no reason to sacrifice
what appears to be a pleasure
for both of us

why should days from now
be considered
when now feels good

is good

pas, 27 November, 1973

yesterday
i told you
i think i will write a poem

you replied
that will only take five minutes

my answer was
not to express the emotions i feel

but today i realized
the poem

is you

pas, 19 January, 1974

knowing you can go home

to someone

who loves you

is what makes life

beautiful

pas, 21 September, 1977

when you are gone
i cease to be
so much you are
a part of me

pas, 21 September, 1977

love like the sunshine
touching the earth
filling with laughter
crying
and birth

birth of understanding
nonself

thus was our companionship
warm

free

pas, 16 October, 1977

you came into my life
like a breeze
of fresh air
suddenly awakening me
from my lethargy

you came into my soul
breathing life
once again

now you come and go
as if allowing us a chance
to regain our breaths
rejuvenate our strength
for the next onslaught
of passion

and in between times
we hungrily
hang on to those moments
of oneness
frightened

you came into my life
with all the warmth of summer
melting the icy bitterness
from my heart

how then shall you leave me

pas, 2 January, 1978

growing up
is learning how to pretend
again

pretending that:

it doesn't matter
if you are all alone

it doesn't matter
if you are a successful
whatever

to love is better
than being loved
or not loving at all

plants need talking to
to grow

we are willows
swaying gracefully in the wind

or that we are musically and harmoniously
part of the universe

or we are papier-maché walruses
sitting quietly in the corner
thinking amusedly upon altruistic obfuscations

that George Washington
only bridged a gap

pretending, more than anything
that words convey feeling

pretending our love is still new

let us pretend again!

pas, 1 October, 1978

the night was filled
with fleeting touches
longing glances that seemed to say
i want to be close to you

the music was intense
full of emotion
recapitulating ours
bouncing it off the walls

we lapsed
into brief moments
of acute awareness
of one another

more often than not driven
to the far reaches of our souls
submerged by the fear
of selflessness

and when we were
finally together
were we not really
alone

pas, 16 October, 1978

today
our sandwiches lie
breast to breast

sharing an intimacy
which we ourselves
sometimes express

ham and cheese on rye
turkey on white

contiguous, tandem

we replicate
in the night

salt and pepper
are sporadically arranged
on each slice

our passion flares

tenderness, possession

we attempt to splice
our separateness

and consume

our lunch

pas, 13 November, 1978

the play
of our minds

adrift
in time
and space

cast rainbows
upon foreign shores

our love
is wafted
away

by our own movements
of torrential serenity

pas, 19 December, 1978

i sense your being
slipping
into that corner
where you keep yourself in check

i sense
pulling away

you speak of justice
in tones of humanity

all i can think
is
why aren't you closer

was it too soon

pas, 27 November, 1979

clouds
shadow-like
glide
across the sand

sun and breeze
caress you
as you drift in
my heart

pas, 20 June, 1979

we are one
you and i

in the sun
and
under the blueness of the sky
we are one
shout we

let it be known
we are one
but free

pas, undated

nightime

rain spattered windows

tears upon my face

longings

firesides

patience

quiet

feelings of love

pas, undated

Reflection

the competitors scowl at one another
in their primitive atmosphere
never realizing that their
private discoveries do
not change the course of the earth, just human events

pride is unjust

pas, June 24,1968

a tormented mind
raging to live

a quiet soul unwilling to give
and dare to dream

words are empty
without meaning

emotions are still
no depth of feeling

but through it all
a heart is beating

pas, 26 January, 1969

long to be free
doing things i want to do
being what i want to be

long to be free
never caring what should be
always feeling what could be

long to be free
free to love with all of me

free to share

pas, 13 March, 1969

once a desert
now fertile soil

entropy
removed by toil

a half-being
becoming whole

once lacking inner peace
now possessing a soul

pas, 15 April, 1969

roads to build, trains to ride, views to see
the wanderer leaves when he pleases
stays when he dares
dreams when there are no dreams
travels where there is no highway
loses what he must win

friends to find, enemies to know, emotions to hide
the wanderer feels when he can
laughs when he should cry

oh wanderer, wanderer, you'll lie awake one night
and find that you
are there

pas, dc, 29 April, 1969

dc = David Creed

words on white paper
in an orderly fashion

words on small paper
reflecting their passion

words on smooth paper
what is their meaning

beautiful words on rough paper

pas, 19 may, 1969

out comes me
slowly
struggling to be
holy

out comes the martyr
that is me
struggling violently
to be free

such divinity

pas, 27 May, 1969

yesterday was rough
now the calm
descends on the weary players

the game ensnared them all
a storm shall surely come
before the fall

for whom will they call

where will they fall
these children who spring from flowers

will they strike the rich bed
from which they were fed
only to play dead

pas, 10 July, 1969

some memories cannot
be cast off
as easily as worn out shoes

some rejections hurt more
than those suffered before

but through it all
love can be stronger
hope resides longer

forevermore

pas, 1 July, 1969

the growing pain of growing

pas, 22 July, 1969

mind is encompassed
with impending doom
must get out of this
place

i call myself

pas, 24 July, 1969

when man opens his eyes
and finds himself vulnerable
to the whims and fantasies
of a world filled with hardness
his mind and soul long to shield
themselves from the blinding light
long to be pushed into the darkness once more
the darkness comforts him

no test of honesty
integrity
no confrontation with reality
immorality

it seems such a contradiction to
fight for reality and survival
but hate the fight
hate reality
and hate being forced to fight to survive

heads pound with words
light
darkness
comfort
honesty
right
downtrodden
spirit
freedom
knowledge

once these words were meaningful
they stood for something
now they reek of ambiguity
desecration--innovation

don't part your hair
don't gain weight
don't be proud
don't smile

lie
then cry
cry to be heard
above the mob of don'ts

scream to be heard
shriek
no response
those who hear already possess honesty
integrity
the others are deaf

let's save a dying company
make its foundation firmer
replace its present one with
tired souls and bruised minds
and take the more creative ones
for cornerstones
the stronger the better
this way the company will not fall
its success will be built upon these
beautiful people

then sit and listen to talk of dignity
ah there's the clue — talk
action is outmoded

there's a lot to be said for man
but there isn't a language descriptive enough

pas, 11 April, 1970

a time will come
when feelings
no longer exist

the mind will house
no emotion
only cold knowledge

and the only contact
man will have with emotion
will be that recorded by
writers and poets

but the unfortunate fact
is that future man
will not recognize
the passion behind the print

pas, 14 July, 1970

closer to reality
fantasy
or nonentity

reactions
that inspire
fear

chemical
or otherwise

pas, 10 November, 1970

oceans away
and worlds apart
drift we
in our obscurity

even the simple
amoeba must have
a stronger
sense of belonging

chasms mended
bricks fall-
the ending?

selling out
giving in
is that what life
is all about

pas, 23 November, 1970

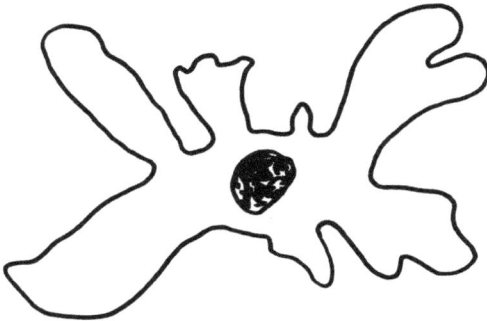

went to the sea
in search of my birth
but found the sea receded

went to the mountains
in search of my youth
but found them aged

went within in search of myself
and found a rainbow

pas, 23 June, 1971

my heart

my soul

and i

do not agree

we should be one

but yet we're three

pas, 3 November, 1971

touch: to feel tactile pleasure

think: to feel touchfully

pas, 13 January, 1972

things have changed

they cannot remain constant

like cells

people cycle

pas, 16 October, 1977

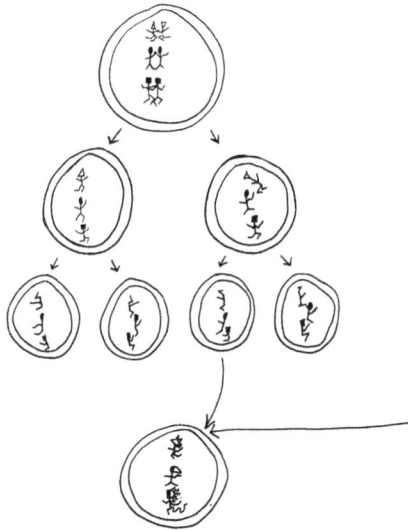

memories only
retard
further development of ones
emotions

pas, 14 November, 1977

and yet we try
as though we must

to delve into life
with gentle thrusts

we seek to touch
to cure
to heal

to communicate ourselves
as real

pas, 15 December, 1977

remembrance of conversation past:

and how have you survived

i replied

fleetingly

pas, 20 December, 1977

once in a while
a person comes along
and there is an easy
manner of talking

and you feel
that no matter
what you say
the person
listens
cares

in spite of all
your fears
you give
freely
fully

thank you
for bringing out
me from me

pas, 13 February, 1978

tonight three people were together
they ate, drank, talked
something beautiful happened
feelings
they went to a pier to fish
rain began falling
felt good...cold and wet

the pensive one lingered
tasting raindrops
becoming dissatisfied with the game
joined the others in the car
a convertible that
the three of them loved, shared, touched

not all appreciate a soft top
but these three loved
the wind blowing
through their hair
the joy of living

he loved the performance of the car
fast
the way it hugged the road
she the air
the speed

the other
loved the world
a world full of
beauty

insensitive

pas, undated

time extends
as tar
covers the cracks
in the pavement

drawing the chasms
closer

time smoothes
the surfaces
of life

sadly removing

the texture

pas, undated

Heartbreak

sadly i searched for love
quickly i lost it

hungrily i yearned for love
more and more i lost it

earnestly i searched for life
wincingly i found it

madly i searched for me

pas, 16 May, 1969

where are you
and
where am I

look
do not see you

touch
do not feel you

does proximity
alone

determine closeness

pas, 19 May, 1969

when i saw the pain
and sorrow in your eyes
i could but wonder
what held back
the skies

a sky once beautiful
now is black
because of truths
turned to lies

truth too quickly
finds disguise
in smaller and
smaller
and whiter
lies

your eyes were filled
with tears unshed
your mouth was filled
with words unsaid

the wall melted slowly
partially
not wholly

pas, 20 June, 1969

my mind is cluttered with withdrawal
what to do
my concern is shallow
what can i do
sympathize, then analyze
but does that help you

my heart hangs heavy outside my soul
it too has not reached its goal
to fulfill must be the key
but i cannot be
the one who makes you free

deep inside you
the answer lies
and like my soul
yours also cries

pas, 24 June, 1969

her song at last is sung
she called it death
the melody gathered her soul
in one soft heap

her trials were many
her sorrows deep

twas a year ago when last i looked
into that unhappy face
wanted to help
tried
but felt no embrace

she grieved inside
finding no escape
from her solitary existence

her loneliness was great
her pain so heavy

but why death did she rate

pas, 21 October, 1969

patience
going forward rapidly
pausing only to look back
waiting

for silence-breaking

wanting
trembling with anticipation
no communication
no barriers broken

feelings stacked

pas, 27 January, 1970

the clouds fell over her eyes
once more

in the height of her passion
she wept
outwardly no within yes

her life had been moved
like so many pawns
in a game of chess

pas, 1 March, 1970

time went by
then the garbage truck came
to collect all the lost words and phrases
throwing them into some semblance of disorder

love was buried beneath piles
of banana peels
grapefruit pulp
and aluminum foil

coke cans (it's the real thing ...)
were stacked on top of
i like you as you are (that's the way it should be)
and other expressions in unknown tongues

meaning was lost the day
the garbage man came

pas, March 8, 1971

at times I care
and sometimes I don't

sometimes I love

and at times I don't

most of the time I suffer from feeling

or lack of it

pas, October 11, 1971

the way you say
how you feel
cuts through the barrier
that only words reveal

pas, 19 February, 1974

woke up this morning with no name
my thoughts were a jumble
things were not plain

i clothed myself in the same fashion
as earlier this year
but my body is different
and my mind yet unclear

i have lost myself

woke up this morning in a dark room
the sun began shining
i wasn't alone

suppressing my thoughts
i ran away
far too soon

i have found myself

woke up this morning
i felt dead
i reached for you
and you were there

i no longer exist

i ran down the street in angry despair
my soul, my soul
are you there

the trees, the pavement, the streetlight
all answered
everywhere

woke up this morning in an effort to rise
climbing ever higher
i need a disguise

pas, 21 August, 1974

my mind and soul are covered in shrouds
my heart aches
from mouthing words
with no meaning

despair runs rampant
battering my emotions
setting a stage of unreality

fear creeps
undulating from the play
of my mind

pas, 16 October, 1977

should i go
will it be harder

merely a delay of healing
will it allay fears

generated by revealing

myself

pas, 16 October, 1977

sure!
all of these aches
and pains
build your character
if...
you can ever
pull yourself
out of the
grief

pas, 14 November, 1977

why am i spilling my guts
all of a sudden

have i gone completely mad

throwing all caution to the wind

can i be so starved for affection
that i'm chasing it away

or is it that the loss is so great

that there is no possible way
to fill the void

yet i still grasp

pas, 5 December, 1977

i can still recall the warmth
of your body
pressed ever so close

and your lips
full and receiving

i cannot drive from my mind
your

essence

pas, 23 January, 1978

i sought you
because i thought
you would be
a worthwhile person
to know

now i find you've
created work to make
the association legal

i'm sorry you need
the excuse

i don't

pas, 5 June, 1978

stars fall
across the sky

and the water
undulates
in the seas

the sun rises
as the rivers run
carrying a special seed
containing
a little something
for me

again
i dip
into life

holding water
in my hands

pas, 19 December, 1978

my love for you
was submerged

so i thought

somewhere in the far reaches
of my heart

i have not touched your soul
your essence
for such a long time

then quite suddenly
you slipped into
my hands again

ah, but i must remember
you are ethereal

again my love
escaped its boundaries

it flows through me
coursing each fiber
until I no longer recognize me

it fills me with such despair

because it lies in state

pas, 6 March, 1979

last night
i dreamed

i dreamed
of fishing poles
being caught
by hooks

losing my coat
searching
from building
to building

finding a lovely
room
in a dark, dank
cellar

meeting a wonderful
little old lady
truly regal
in appearance and tastes

her daughter
who was ill
with some disease
of the joints

and I came
to save them

lost in feelings
of true love
and compassion

then
while cycling

back and forth
from writings
and rambling
i was struck
by a truck
in a crowded
intersection

my courage
was not daunted

I rushed home
to my loved ones

but they were gone

was not my dream
reality

pas, 7 January, 1979

tears tried to flow
last night

but instead caught upon
my cheeks like

dried rainflakes

the barriers were not broken

not quite there

pas, 4 September, 1979

Whimsy

found a horse in the mail today
reminded me of a day filled with a sandy beach
and warmth

it now stands on a shelf with other treasures
driftwood, an owl, and a pine cone

even the tiniest of creatures has meaning

pas, 6 March, 1969

butterflies usually fly in the sky

mine hide in my stomach

oh my

wish mine were free to fly

pas, 7 March, 1969

the enzyme is repairing like mad
oh
won't the dna be glad

it suffered a cruel fate
all warm and damp
exposed to a uv lamp

and now it is damaged
all full of dimers
but wait a minute
is it trimers

yet dna never fear
ye ole pr enzyme is near

pas, 2 July, 1969

pr = photoreactivating

spirits are high
might even fly

through the sky

pas, 8 July, 1969

when one considers possibilities
enthusiasm prevails

but when probablities are possible
eagerness converts to boredom

pas, 4 March, 1971

the poet
the cynic
they're one and the same
one calls them by flowers
the other calls them by name

pas, 29 August, 1971

men are a compilation
of all they see
read
or touch

words

pas, 13 January, 1972

a checker in a groc. store
is what i wanta be
10 cents here
how much is tea

a simple life
with vegetables

pas, 5 October, 1972

there was a time i thought
i would write poetry for a living
then realized it was poetry
for living

pas, 2 February, 1973

a shell is made
for putting to your ear
to hear

a shell is hollow inside

pas, 26 March, 1973

allusion

elusion

delusion

all pertinent words

in a soul search

pas, 3 January, 1974

it is fall in the north
all the leaves declare
a little nip in the air

they blush
in happy anticipation
to see the trees naked

pas, 16 October, 1977

there's something comforting
about smoking a pipe
perhaps it's the beauty
of the slender stem
enunciated by the bowl

no, more than that
it's the smooth feel
of the wood
and the sensuous draw
of smoke

curling into the mouth

pas, 23 January, 1978

sitting in a daze
most curiously

undergoing transcendental
morphogenesis

thoughts of another time
now meaningless

words with another rhyme
how humorous

tangential expression
of a new era

pas, 22 September, 1978

retribution

that insensate leveler of humanity
has finally caught up with his quarry

in one to one stoichiometry
he struck once again

without piety

pas, 6 October, 1978

put a purpose in your life today

it's sold on
every street corner less than a
block away

10¢ here
a dollar there

                                        pas, undated

it has been told
in days of old
that things of gold
glitter

but I find
that other things shine
and gold
only
flitters

pas, undated

Phyllis Ann Shaw, Ph.D. is a tenured Associate Professor at the Icahn School of Medicine at Mount Sinai. This volume is a collection of her poems covering a span of a few decades and deals with a changing horizon of the human condition. This very personal collection represents a literary debut for the author. Dr. Shaw, a native Texan, has been a long term resident of Manhattan.

www.ingramcontent.com/pod-product-compliance
Lightning Source LLC
Chambersburg PA
CBHW022307060426
42446CB00007BA/742